W9-BII-379

Transportation & Communication Series

Telephones

Joanne Mattern

Enslow Publishers, Inc.

40 Industrial Road   PO Box 38
Box 398   Aldershot
Berkeley Heights, NJ 07922   Hants GU12 6BP
USA   UK

http://www.enslow.com

Copyright © 2002 by Enslow Publishers, Inc.

All rights reserved.

No part of this book may be reproduced by any means
without the written permission of the publisher.

Library of Congress Cataloging-in-Publication Data

Mattern, Joanne, 1963-
    Telephones / Joanne Mattern.
        p. cm. — (Transportation & communication series)
    Includes bibliographical references and index.
    ISBN 0-7660-1888-1
    1. Telephone—Juvenile literature. [1. Telephone.] I. Title. II.
Transportation and communication series.
TK6165 .M38 2002
621.385—dc21   2001001779

Printed in the United States of America

10 9 8 7 6 5 4 3 2 1

To Our Readers: We have done our best to make sure all Internet addresses in this book were active
and appropriate when we went to press. However, the author and the publisher have no control over and
assume no liability for the material available on those Internet sites or on other Web sites they may link
to. Any comments or suggestions can be sent by e-mail to comments@enslow.com or to the address on
the back cover.

Every effort has been made to locate all copyright holders of material used in this book. If any errors or
omissions have occurred, corrections will be made in future editions of this book.

Illustration Credits: AP Photo, p. 6; AP Photo/Patricia McDonnell, p. 40; AP Photo/
Columbia Daily Tribune/Don Shrubshell, p. 34; AP Photo/David Zalubowski, p. 38; Courtesy
of the Bancroft Library, p. 16; Canadian Heritage-Parks Canada, Alexander Graham Bell
National Historic Site, Baddeck, Nova Scotia, pp. 30 (top), 32, 33 (bottom); Corel
Corporation, pp. 8, 17, 27, 42; The Denver Public Library, Western History Collection, pp.
19, 22; Dover Publications, Inc., p. 5; Enslow Publishers, Inc., pp. 13, 18, 20; Gilbert H.
Grosvenor Collection, Library of Congress, p. 31; Hemera Technologies, Inc. 1997–2000,
pp. 1, 2, 9, 11, 12, 13 (picture of phone), 15, 26, 29, 30 (bottom), 35, 39, 41, 42 (top,
snowshoes); Library of Congress, pp. 4, 7, 10, 14, 21, 23, 24, 28, 33 (top), 36, 37; NASA,
p. 25.

Cover Illustrations: Hemera Technologies, Inc. 1997–2000.

CENTRAL ARKANSAS LIBRARY SYSTEM
SIDNEY S. McMATH BRANCH LIBRARY
LITTLE ROCK, ARKANSAS

Contents

"I Hear! I Hear!"

Alexander Graham Bell

On Sunday, June 25, 1876, a group of judges were in Philadelphia, Pennsylvania. It was their job to pick the most important and exciting invention at the Centennial Exposition. This show was like a giant fair. It would show off the best inventions in the United States. It was called the Centennial Exposition because it had been one hundred years since the United States was founded.

At the far end of the hall, a man named Alexander Graham Bell waited for the judges to see his invention. His invention let two people talk to each other over a distance. It

To the left is a view of the grounds and buildings of the 1876 Centennial Exposition.

used electricity to send voices over wires. The invention was called the telephone.

Bell had not wanted to show his telephone. He did not think it was good enough to win. But his friends talked him into showing it.

Bell watched the judges come his way. It took a long time for them to look at all the different inventions. Bell and his telephone were tucked away in a corner. The judges did not even see him. It was such a hot day that the judges were about to stop looking and go home.

One of the judges was Dom Pedro II, the emperor, or leader, of Brazil. Dom Pedro had met Bell before. Suddenly, Dom Pedro looked up and saw Bell at the far end of the hall. He told the other judges that they must see Bell's invention.

Bell asked each of the judges to listen to the receiver of his telephone. Then Bell walked to

One of Bell's first telephones looked like this.

a transmitter at the other end of the hall. He spoke into the transmitter.

When Dom Pedro picked up the receiver, he was surprised to hear Bell's voice coming out of it, loud and clear. The emperor jumped up and yelled, "I hear! I hear!"

Alexander Graham Bell's telephone became the most popular invention at the Exposition.

People gather at the opening ceremonies. The Centennial Exposition also had parades to celebrate the United States turning 100 in 1876 (inset).

How Telephones Work

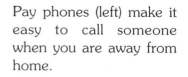

A telephone is easy to use. To make a call, a person just picks up the receiver and pushes some buttons on the base unit. To answer the phone, the person picks up the receiver and talks into it. But a telephone is not as simple as it looks. Wires, switches, and computers work together to make talking on the telephone possible.

Numbers and Frequencies

The first step in making a telephone call is dialing the number. Each number makes a set of vibrations, which is called a frequency. These vibrations create a sound called a tone.

Pay phones (left) make it easy to call someone when you are away from home.

This is a later model of Bell's telephone.

Each tone has a different frequency. Vibrations are back-and-forth movements created by sound. This lets the telephone equipment tell one number from another.

Each tone sends an electrical signal through the telephone wire. The signal moves along the wires to a telephone pole. At the telephone pole, the signal runs down a wire into the ground. There it moves along a bigger telephone wire. This big wire is called a cable.

The telephone cable ends in a building called a switching office. At the switching

office, a computer called a tone decoder listens to the signals. Each frequency tells the decoder to open a special set of electrical circuits. These circuits, or paths, then send a signal to the phone that is being called. A separate electrical signal also moves down the wires. This signal rings the bell on the phone to tell the person he or she has a phone call.

Speaking Electrically

Once someone answers the phone, another set of electrical signals is sent between the two phones. These signals deliver the sounds that make up the voices of the two people who are talking.

Telephones let people talk to others who live far away.

A person's voice does not move over the wires and into the phone on the other end. Instead, the voice is changed into a series of electrical signals.

Every telephone has a transmitter and a receiver. The transmitter sends

Early phones did not look like the phones we have today.

electrical signals along the wires. The receiver gets the signals.

When a person talks, the voice produces sound waves. The transmitter inside the phone takes these sound waves and changes them into electrical signals. Because each sound wave has a different frequency, each electrical signal is different too.

Transmitters have a special piece of metal called a diaphragm. Sound waves make the diaphragm vibrate. The diaphragm is filled with tiny grains of carbon. As the diaphragm vibrates, the carbon moves around. The movement of the carbon creates electrical signals. These electrical signals are sent through the wires. They travel to the receiver of the phone on the other end of the connection.

Receivers also have a diaphragm. When electrical signals come into the phone, the receiver's diaphragm vibrates. These vibrations turn the electrical signals back into sound waves. These sound waves sound just like the person's voice.

Sending and receiving sound waves usually takes less than a second. This speed makes it easy for two people to talk to each other over the telephone. Before the telephone was invented, this type of communication was not so easy.

The handset of a phone has a transmitter and a receiver. All these parts let us talk to people who live next door, in another state, or even in another country.

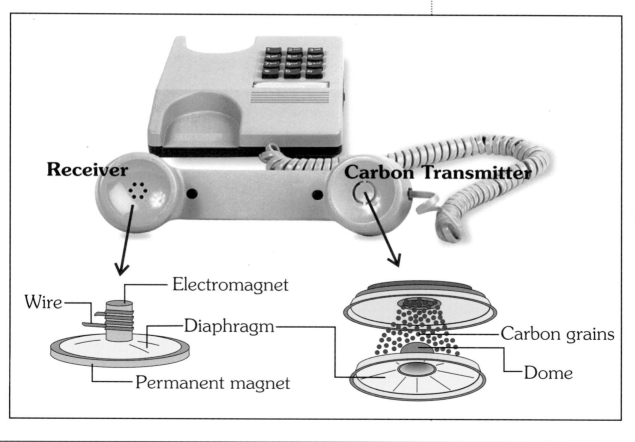

Receiver

Carbon Transmitter

Wire

Electromagnet

Diaphragm

Permanent magnet

Carbon grains

Dome

History of the Telephone

Before the telephone, there were few ways to communicate with people who lived far away. The most simple way was to write a letter. Writing a letter let people share news with friends and family almost anywhere in the country or the world.

But there were many problems when sending a letter. The biggest problem was that it took a long time for letters to travel from one person to another. Two hundred years ago, letters were often carried on stagecoaches. Some letters were sent on ships. Others were given to travelers who

An early telephone (left).

passed through town. These travelers would pass the letter along to other travelers they met. It could take months for a letter to travel this way. Letters were often lost in storms or accidents.

In 1860, the Pony Express began. Young men carried the mail on horseback. Each man carried a sack of mail about twenty-five miles. Then another rider took over and traveled another twenty-five miles. The Pony Express

Pony Express riders had to ride their horses in all kinds of weather.

could deliver a letter from St. Joseph, Missouri, to Sacramento, California, in about ten days. This was very fast in those days. But the Pony Express had problems too. Riders were often attacked by robbers or wild animals. They also had to face bad weather, such as floods and snowstorms.

Pony Express riders were sometimes attacked by robbers or wild animals.

The Telegraph

The Pony Express only lasted eighteen months. There was a new invention called the telegraph. The telegraph put the Pony Express out of business.

Years earlier, in 1832, a man named Samuel Morse began looking for a way to send messages through electrical signals. In 1844, Morse sent the first telegraph message from Washington, D.C., to Baltimore, Maryland.

Like the telephone, the telegraph sent messages by wire over long distances. The messages were sent in Morse code over wires by electricity. Morse code uses short and long sounds combined in various ways to stand for letters, numerals, and other characters. A short sound is called a dit, and a long sound is called a dah. People who understood Morse code had to decode the dits and dahs and turn them back into words. It was like working a puzzle.

Before the telephone, people sometimes sent telegraph messages using Morse code. Morse code uses dits (dots or ●) and dahs (dashes or —) that stand for letters and numbers.

Telegraph operators put the dits and dahs together. Then they sent the message.

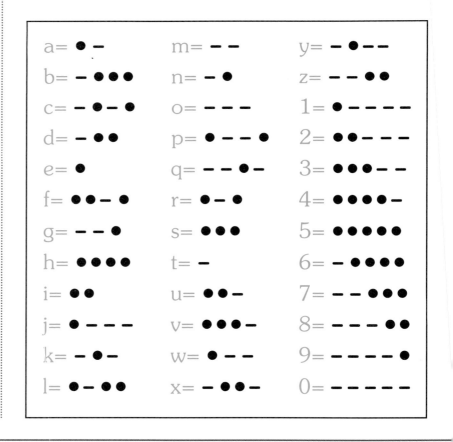

a= ● —	m= — —	y= — ● — —
b= — ● ● ●	n= — ●	z= — — ● ●
c= — ● — ●	o= — — —	1= ● — — — —
d= — ● ●	p= ● — — ●	2= ● ● — — —
e= ●	q= — — ● —	3= ● ● ● — —
f= ● ● — ●	r= ● — ●	4= ● ● ● ● —
g= — — ●	s= ● ● ●	5= ● ● ● ● ●
h= ● ● ● ●	t= —	6= — ● ● ● ●
i= ● ●	u= ● ● —	7= — — ● ● ●
j= ● — — —	v= ● ● ● —	8= — — — ● ●
k= — ● —	w= ● — —	9= — — — — ●
l= ● — ● ●	x= — ● ● —	0= — — — — —

These men are working in a telegraph office in 1915.

Telegraph wires were soon laid across the United States. Later, a cable was laid under the Atlantic Ocean to send messages to other parts of the world. Sending messages by telegraph was much faster than sending them by mail.

Even though the telegraph was fast, it had a lot of problems. The telegraph used special machines that could not be put in people's homes. If a person wanted to send a telegram,

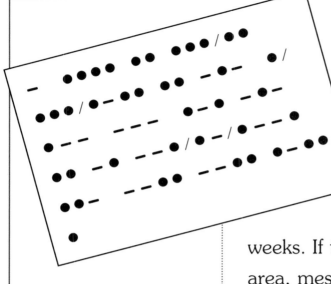

Use the Morse code chart on page 18 to decode this message. The answer is on page 44. The slashes (/) separate the words.

he or she had to go to the telegraph office. When a message was received at the telegraph office, someone had to write down the message. Then the message had to be delivered. This could take several hours or several weeks. If there were no telegraph cables in an area, messages could not be sent there.

Because telegraph messages were sent in Morse code, most people could not send messages themselves. They had to find a telegraph operator to send the message for them.

It was also difficult to send a telegraph message to other countries. The United States used a system called American Morse. The rest of the world used International Morse. Because these two codes were different, telegraph operators in other countries could not always understand messages from America.

The Early Days of the Telephone

The telegraph made communicating much easier. But many people thought there might be a better way to send messages. In 1876, Alexander Graham Bell invented the telephone. By the end of the 1800s, telephone wires were replacing telegraph wires all over the country.

Alexander Graham Bell's telephone looks different from the phones used today. This man is showing how to use Bell's first telephone.

In the early days of the telephone, all calls went through a switchboard, like the one seen here.

Using the telephone in the late 1800s was not like using it today. Telephone wires only covered short distances. There was no such thing as a long-distance call because the sound waves were not strong enough to travel very far away.

In the early days of the telephone, all calls went through a switchboard. When a person wanted to make a call, he picked up the phone and talked to an operator. He told the operator what number he wanted to call.

The operator sat at the switchboard and connected the wires to put the call through. It was not until many years later that telephones came with dials. This allowed people to make phone calls themselves instead of going through an operator.

Receiving a telephone call was different too. Every community used party lines. Several houses were on the same phone line. When someone received a call, every phone on the line would ring. Each house had a special ring to tell the people that the call was for them. But anyone on the party line could pick up the phone and listen to the conversation. Beginning in 1946, houses were given their own telephone numbers.

Changes to the Telephone

In 1904, a way was discovered to amplify signals, or make them stronger. This made long-distance calling possible. In 1914, underground cables connected large cities

Before individual phone numbers, communities used party lines. Houses were on the same phone line. Each house had a different ring, but everyone on that party line could pick up their phone and listen to the conversation. This poster is suggesting people should not tell secrets on a party line.

Perhaps it would be better if I just whispered the next bit...

DON'T DISCUSS SECRETS ON THE TELEPHONE

23

such as Boston, New York, and Washington, D.C. By 1915, telephone lines connected the East and West coasts of the United States.

In 1956, the first telephone cable was laid under the Atlantic Ocean. This let people in the United States make and receive phone calls from Europe and Asia. But there were not enough cables to carry a lot of calls at the same time. If a person in New York wanted to call someone in Paris, France, she had to call the long-distance operator. The operator

In 1915, the first trans-continental phone line was installed. It connected the East and West coasts of the United States. The first transcontinental call was made from Washington, D.C.

would put the call through when a cable was open. A person might wait hours or even days for a call to go through. These connections were not very good, and it could be hard to hear what the other person was saying.

In 1945, science-fiction writer Arthur C. Clarke thought of using satellites in space to send telephone signals. Seventeen years later, in 1962, the first telecommunications satellite, Telstar, was put into orbit. Satellites let long-distance calls go through quickly and easily. They also made the sound quality better, so people could hear each other more clearly.

By the 1970s, push-button phones were beginning to replace dial telephones. Pushing a button helped send signals faster. This let phone calls be made more quickly and easily, too.

Today's Telephone
Today's telephone is very different from the one used in the late 1800s. The only thing a

Communication satellites make sound quality better when people talk on the phone.

An answering machine (top) and cordless phone (below).

phone could do then was send and receive messages.

Today, telephones are used in most parts of the world. People just dial a number to speak to anyone they want to quickly. Cordless phones let people move around as they talk. Cell phones let people make phone calls without being connected by wires.

Telephones also make it easy to call for help in an emergency. Most neighborhoods are part of the 911 system. If a person needs to call the police, fire department, or ambulance, he or she does not have to look up these phone numbers. Instead, he or she simply dials 911. The call is quickly sent to an emergency operator, or dispatcher, who will send help.

Phones have many handy features. They include voice mail to record messages if a person is not able to answer the phone. Caller ID has a screen that displays the name and number of the person who is calling. Redial and memory features dial numbers automatically, instead of the caller having to punch in the numbers. Telephones have made communication around the world as easy as pushing a few buttons.

This dispatcher (below) is answering an emergency call. Most neighborhoods today belong to the 911 emergency system.

Alexander Graham Bell

Who was the man who changed the world by inventing the telephone? His name was Alexander Graham Bell. Bell was interested in communicating with the deaf. The invention of the telephone happened because of Bell's work with the deaf.

Deaf people cannot hear normally. Some people are born deaf. Others become deaf because of an illness or an accident. If a person is born deaf or becomes deaf as a baby, the person probably will not be able to talk normally. That is because a person needs to hear sounds and words in order to make the

Alexander Graham Bell began experimenting with electricity and wires in 1875. His lab was in this building (left) in Boston, Massachusetts.

Alexander Graham Bell.

sounds themselves. For this reason, many deaf people communicate through sign language. They use their fingers to make symbols for words instead of talking.

Alexander Graham Bell was born in Edinburgh, Scotland, on March 3, 1847. His mother was deaf. Bell communicated with her by speaking close to her forehead. He thought that his mother could "hear" him by picking up the vibrations of his voice.

Bell was very interested in how voices made sounds. He thought these sounds could be sent through wires by using electricity. Later, Bell would use his ideas about vibrations and electricity when he worked on the telephone.

When he was twenty-three, Bell and his parents moved to Ontario, Canada. A year later, Bell began teaching deaf children at a school in Boston, Massachusetts. He taught them to talk using a system his father had invented. This system was called Visible

Speech. It used symbols to show students how the throat, tongue, and lips moved to produce certain sounds. Bell later married one of his students, Mabel Hubbard.

At the same time he was teaching, Bell was also looking for a way to send sound waves over long distances. He began working with Thomas Watson. The two men tried to change sound waves into electrical signals and send them over a wire.

On March 10, 1876, Bell accidentally spilled battery acid onto his pants. He called out, "Mr. Watson, come here. I want you." Watson, who was working in another room, heard Bell's voice over a wire. Bell's ideas about sending sound waves through a wire had worked.

Bell showed his new invention at the Centennial Exposition in Philadelphia, Pennsylvania, in June 1876. Scientists and people everywhere were excited by this new invention. In 1878, Rutherford B. Hayes

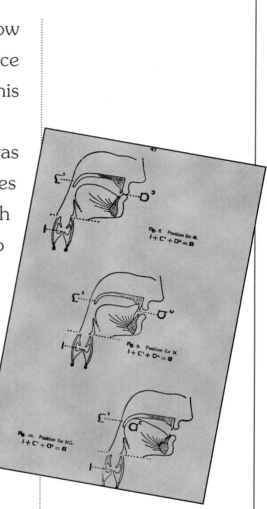

Bell used a system called Visible Speech. It used symbols to show students how the throat, tongue, and lips moved to produce certain sounds.

Thomas Watson helped Bell with his telephone experiments.

Mabel Hubbard, shown here at age 14, married Alexander Graham Bell.

became the first United States president to put a telephone in the White House. Although other scientists had worked on telephones, Bell was the first to register his invention with the United States Patent Office. Today, Bell is known as the inventor of the telephone.

Bell invented several other things, including an electrical probe to find bullets in the human body. He also gave money to groups interested in science to help them come up with new inventions. He died on August 2, 1922.

Bell Telephone Company

In 1877, Bell founded the Bell Telephone Company and began to sell his new invention. Later, Bell Telephone became the American Telephone and Telegraph Company, or AT&T. Throughout the 1900s, Bell Laboratories and AT&T invented new technologies to make talking on the telephone easier and better.

Bell drew many diagrams with his ideas on how the telephone would work.

Today, Alexander Graham Bell is known as the inventor of the telephone.

Telephone's New Careers

The telephone not only gave people a new way to communicate, it also gave them new jobs and new businesses.

The Human Touch

The first jobs created by the invention of the telephone were telephone operators. Thousands of people were hired to put through calls. Many of these operators were women. During the late 1800s and early 1900s, there were few jobs open to women. Becoming a telephone operator was the first chance for many women to have a job and make money.

The telephone gave people the chance to have new jobs. This telephone lineman (left) is fixing a telephone line.

To make a phone call in the early years of the telephone, people had to call through a switchboard operator. The operator would then connect them to the right person.

Today, computers and other machines put through phone calls. However, many people still help callers look up numbers or solve problems with their telephones.

Many men and women work as telephone installers and repairers. They go into homes to put in telephone lines and other equipment. They also keep the millions of miles of telephone cables that connect homes and businesses all over the country working.

Doing Business

Many companies do business over the phone. Perhaps the most common are telemarketers. Telemarketers call people and try to sell them services or products. These people are able to do their work by phone.

Other companies perform telephone surveys. They call people and ask them questions about a product, experience, or issue. Then they use their answers to measure how much people like a product, or how they feel about important people or events.

The telephone has also created a whole new industry through the Internet. Many companies sell products and services over the Internet. Because the Internet is made up of computers connected by telephone lines, Internet businesses could not exist without the telephone.

This phone book shows the numbers of different locations in the area of the person's home. To make a call, the person would pick up the phone and tell the operator what number they wanted, then the operator would connect the caller.

Chapter 6

Telephones and the Future

The telephone has changed a lot in the past 125 years. Perhaps the greatest development in the past few years has been the mobile, or cellular phone (also called a cell phone). These phones are wireless. Instead of sending signals through wires, cell phones use radio waves to transmit signals. The first mobile phone was invented in 1945. But the technology was not good enough for cell phones to be used by the general public until the 1990s.

New Technologies

People do not use telephones only to talk to each other. The telephone has also started new technologies.

Cell phones use radio waves to transmit signals. Instead of wires, cell phones are connected with the help of cell towers (left).

New ways of using the telephone are being invented everyday. This type of video phone lets deaf children talk to each other using American Sign Language. They can see each other by watching the monitor.

One of the first inventions to use telephone technology was the fax machine. Instead of changing sound waves into electrical signals and sending them over wires, fax machines change pictures into electrical signals. By using a fax machine, a person can transmit, or send, a letter, photo, or drawing to another fax machine anywhere in the world. A person

using a fax machine can send a document in just a few minutes.

Another new technology that uses the telephone is the computer modem. A modem is a telephone inside a computer. Modems let computers "talk" to each other, just like people talk to each other over the telephone. Because computers can "talk" to each other, e-mail and the Internet are possible. Today, one computer can send an e-mail message to another computer in just a few seconds.

Computers with modems allow people to be able to have e-mail and access to the Internet.

People can also link their computer modems to the World Wide Web on the Internet. On the Web, people can find information on just about any topic. They can link to libraries and schools anywhere in the world. They can buy products, play games, and find new friends. None of these things could have happened without the telephone.

The telephone has made the world a different place. It gave people the chance to communicate with anyone, anytime, anywhere, and in any way. It has truly changed the way people live, work, and play.

The telephone lets us talk to people from Alaska to Egypt.

Timeline

1876—Alexander Graham Bell invents the telephone.

1877—Bell forms the Bell Telephone Company.

1904—A way is found to amplify signals, making long-distance calls possible.

1914—Underground cables link Boston, New York, and Washington, D.C.

1915—Telephone cables link the East and West coasts of the United States.

1945—Writer Arthur C. Clarke suggests using communications satellites; the mobile phone is invented.

1946—Individual telephone numbers are issued.

1956—The first telephone cable is laid under the Atlantic Ocean.

1962—The United States launches Telstar, the first active communications satellite.

Timeline

1969—The Internet (then called ARPANET) is created as a way for scientists at different universities to work together.

1971—The first e-mail is sent.

1980s—The fax machine becomes popular.

1989—The World Wide Web is created.

1990s—Cellular, or mobile, telephones become popular.

Answer to the Morse Code message on page 20:
This is like working a puzzle.

Words to Know

amplify—To make something louder or stronger.

cable—A thick wire.

circuit—The path of an electrical signal.

communicate—To share or pass along feelings, thoughts, or information.

diaphragm—A piece of metal that vibrates in a telephone transmitter or receiver.

frequency—The number of times a sound wave vibrates in one second.

modem—The part of a computer used to send information over telephone lines.

party line—A group of houses on one telephone line.

receiver—The part of a telephone that changes electrical signals into sound waves.

switchboard—A panel that connects different telephone lines.

Words to Know

switching office—The central building where telephone calls are connected.

telemarketer—Someone who sells goods or services over the telephone.

tone—A single sound.

tone decoder—A machine that can tell different frequencies apart and make telephone connections.

transmitter—The part of a telephone that changes sound waves into electrical signals.

Learn More About
Telephones

Books

Alphin, Elaine Marie. *Telephones*. Minneapolis, Minn.: Lerner Publishing Group, 2001.

Fisher, Leonard Everett. *Alexander Graham Bell*. New York, N.Y.: Atheneum Books for Young Readers, 1999.

Gearhart, Sarah. *The Telephone*. New York: Atheneum Books for Young Readers, 1999.

Internet Addresses

Brain Spin: Alexander Graham Bell

<http://www.att.com/technology/forstudents/ brainspin/alexbell/>

This is a fun site about Alexander Graham Bell. Get information and play games.

How Stuff Works

<http://www.howstuffworks.com/telephone.htm>

Learn how telephones work.

Index